Bird
In
Hand

A True Story

Nadia and Teri Nowak
Illustrated by Teri Nowak

Riverhouse Press
Portland, Oregon

Riverhouse Press
2020 8th Avenue, PMB 284
West Linn, Oregon 97068
riverhousepress@aol.com

For Andrew,
whose house spider catch-and-release program
taught us to respect all things living,
no matter how small.

When Andrew stepped out on the patio of his home on a warm, clear August morning, he had no idea that he and his wife were about to be caught up in a wonderful adventure. Teri and Andrew enjoyed living in their little house by the Willamette River. On warm days they sat outside on their patio and watched the wild animals hunt, eat and play.

There was a pond next to their house in which fish wove in and out among the roots of the water lilies that floated on the surface. Behind the pond was a bluff full of Himalayan blackberries for the wild creatures to feast upon. On cold, rainy days they could see the river rise and the fog nestle softly in the trees that surrounded them.

They loved being visited by bald eagles, blue herons, hawks, and ospreys who took turns perching on the tall, bare branches of the sturdy old snag at the river's edge and looked out over the busy life on the water.

Andrew and Teri also loved watching the smaller birds, particularly the hummingbirds buzzing around them and drinking sugar water from the bird feeder hanging on the patio. The hummingbirds reminded them of Andrew's father. He believed that the tiny flyers brought good luck. Every time they came to visit, the day was brightened.

That August morning, while the air was still cool, but held the hint of a hot day ahead, Andrew decided it would be refreshing to let the summer breeze flow through the house. He went out to the garage to get the window screens out of winter storage. As he started to remove them he heard a soft rustling. There on the floor, between two screens, he spotted a small, fuzzy, dark ball.

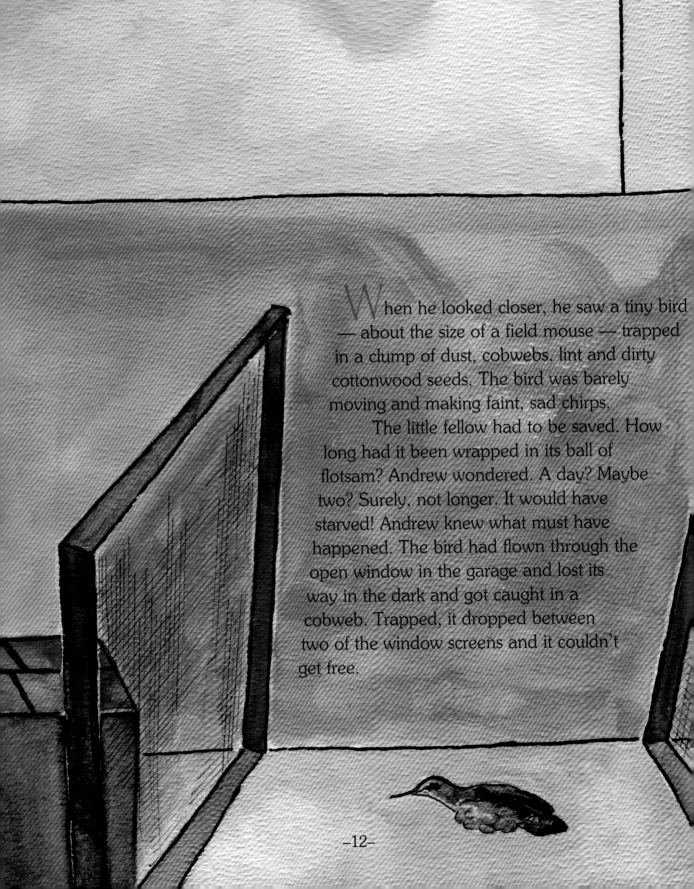

When he looked closer, he saw a tiny bird
— about the size of a field mouse — trapped
in a clump of dust, cobwebs, lint and dirty
cottonwood seeds. The bird was barely
moving and making faint, sad chirps.

The little fellow had to be saved. How
long had it been wrapped in its ball of
flotsam? Andrew wondered. A day? Maybe
two? Surely, not longer. It would have
starved! Andrew knew what must have
happened. The bird had flown through the
open window in the garage and lost its
way in the dark and got caught in a
cobweb. Trapped, it dropped between
two of the window screens and it couldn't
get free.

Gently, Andrew picked up the poor little bundle of feathers and saw that it was a tiny hummingbird. He was amazed that it was still alive —so weak that it was barely breathing. Could it be saved? He had to try. Andrew stepped through the garage door and called to Teri, "Come quick. I need your help!"

When Teri saw the bird in Andrew's hand, she said, "Ahh, poor thing, is it alive?"

"Just barely, but we've got to save it," he said.

"I don't know if we can. It looks too far gone."

"Maybe, but we've got to try."

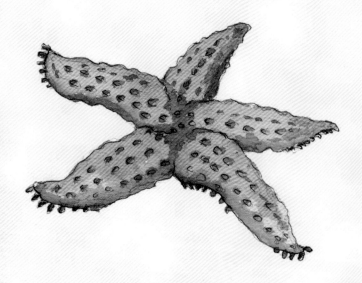

On their way back to the house with the bird cupped gently in Andrew's hand, Teri reminded him of the wounded sea gull they had found at the Oregon coast. The battered creature with an injured wing was struggling to fly, but could not lift off the sandy beach. They decided to catch him, make a splint for his broken wing, then release him when he was healed.

"Don't you remember how frightened that gull was when you picked him up, Andrew? He was so scared that his heart stopped and he died in your hands. What will happen," Teri asked, "if this little bird gets well enough to be frightened? Maybe it's better to let nature take its course."

Andrew shook his head. He insisted on doing something to help even if it seemed hopeless.

After all, the tiny hummingbird still clung to a spark of life. If they could get it to eat, it might live. They had learned that hummingbirds needed to eat at least half of their body weight in food every day to stay healthy. In the house, while Andrew held the bird, Teri mixed some sugar water and poured it into the extra hummingbird feeder they had in the kitchen. Andrew carefully placed the bird's beak into one of the feeder holes. The bird did not move. It was still too weak and dazed to help itself. Their hearts ached for the delicate creature. They knew it would die unless they found a better way to feed it.

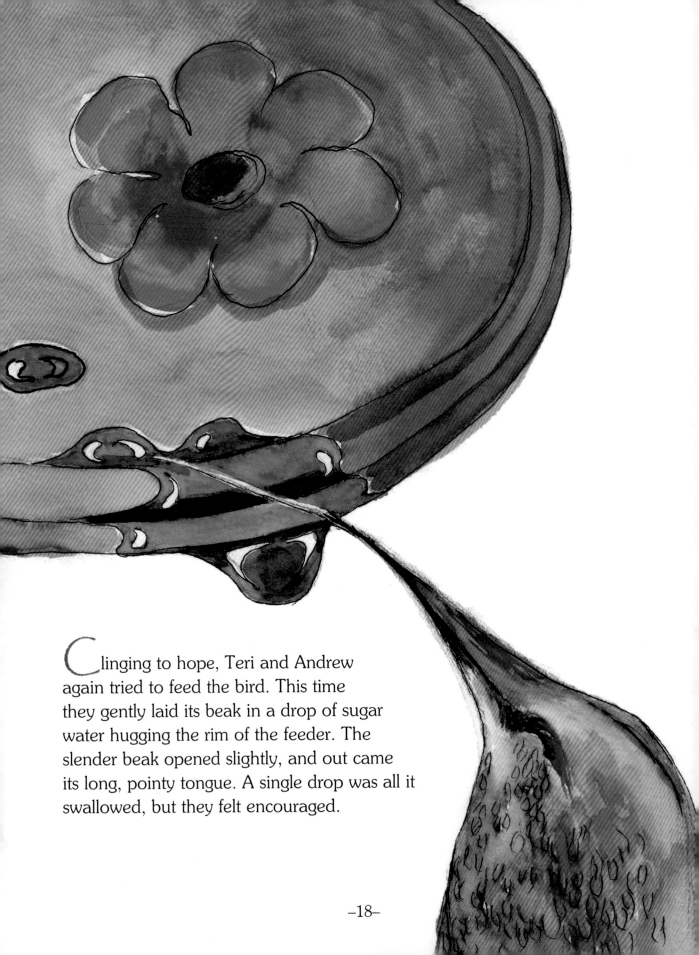

Clinging to hope, Teri and Andrew again tried to feed the bird. This time they gently laid its beak in a drop of sugar water hugging the rim of the feeder. The slender beak opened slightly, and out came its long, pointy tongue. A single drop was all it swallowed, but they felt encouraged.

For the next half hour they helped the bird eat and waited while it rested. It soon began to drink the sugar water more often. When it licked a drop on Andrew's fingertip, he said, "I bet there aren't many people who can tell you what a hummingbird's tongue feels like. Well, I'll tell you. It wiggles and it tickles, and it's scratchy like a cat's tongue."

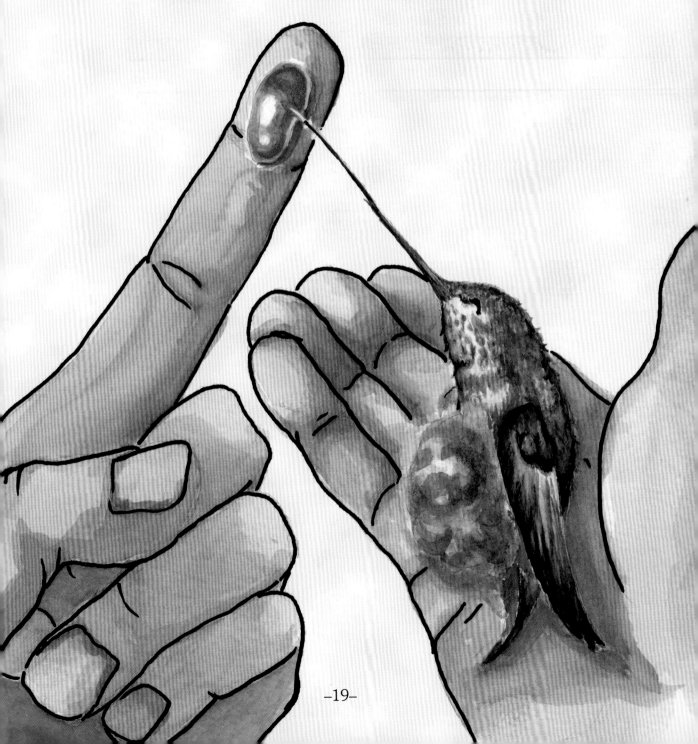

The bird's eyes were tightly shut, and when they opened to take a peek the bird saw two huge faces staring down.
"I'd be scared too if I saw two giants staring down at me," Andrew said when the bird clamped its eyes firmly shut again.

Andrew and Teri knew they had a better chance of untangling the bird if it felt more relaxed. Luckily, Teri remembered a veterinarian had once told her that the best way to relax a bird was to put it on its back. That was exactly what they did, and it worked!

While lying on its back in the palm of Andrew's hand, the humming-bird dropped off to sleep. As Teri looked down at the bird, she could see no sign of its legs. With a small, sharp knife, she carefully cut away the tangle of dirt and debris that bound up the bird and hid its claws. As the bird relaxed its grip, she used a dental pick and some tweezers to free its spindly legs.

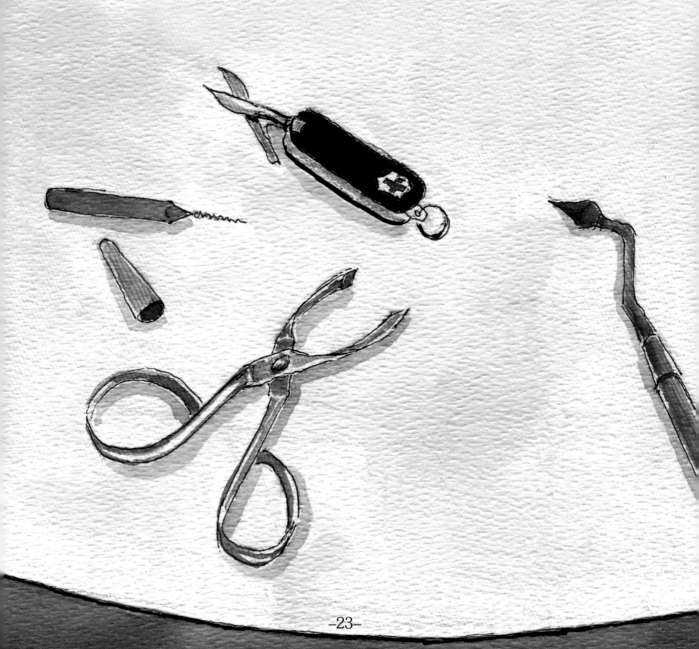

With a damp tissue, Teri wiped the bird clean. Except for some ruffled feathers, the hummingbird looked pretty good.

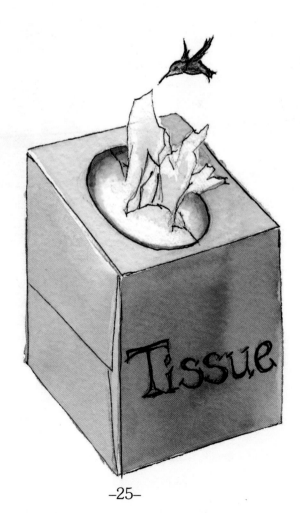

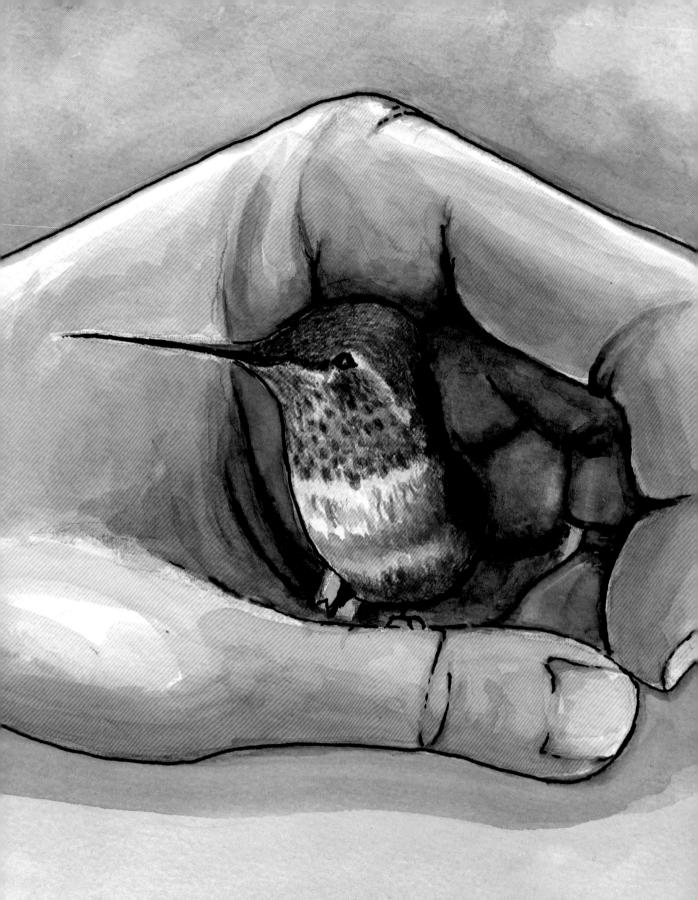

ow that the bird had been freed from its
trap of webs and cotton, Andrew stood it up in
his hand. "The hummingbird seems to trust us,"
he said as the little critter nestled into the warm
hollow of his hand. Andrew could feel the faint
beat of the little bird's heart on his skin. Once
again, he guided the bird's beak gently into the
feeder hole. This time he and Teri could see its
throat moving as it gulped down the sugar water.

Certain that the bird was going to get well, Teri got out their bird book to learn more about their feathered guest. By comparing the size of the bird, as well as the colors and the patterns on its feathers to the pictures in the book, she concluded that their new friend was a female Rufous humming-bird.

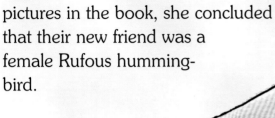

Deciding that they should give their new friend a name, they asked themselves what their kids would have called their visitor. When they were younger, the kids had named their cat Purr and their parakeet Tweety, so Teri and Andrew thought that Hummy was a proper fit.

After two and a half hours of resting and eating, Hummy began to open her eyes. Often she looked straight at Teri and Andrew. They could sense that she was thankful, and trusted her human friends. They too felt a special connection to the beautiful, fragile flyer, who was improving by the minute. Soon, Hummy was able to sit upright.

Andrew, who had been holding the hummingbird for almost three hours, needed to rest his
arm. "I'll just set Hummy on the table for a
little while."

Left alone, she toppled over
like a wooden statue.

Chuckling about how funny she looked when she fell over, Andrew placed her back on his hand.

Soon, Hummy was strong enough to stand on her own. Andrew let her perch on his thumb. She liked it so much that when he stood her on the table again to test her strength, she climbed right back into the safety of his hand.

Teri and Andrew could see that Hummy was beginning to feel strong enough to look at the feeder …

At the forest around them …

And at her new friends without fright.

-33-

By the
third hour, Andrew
needed to rest his arm, so
Teri took the hummingbird into
her hands. As she sat gazing at
Hummy, she couldn't help feeling a
sense of honor that a bird so small could be
so brave and trusting. At that moment, she felt
at peace.

hen Teri had a thought. Wouldn't it be fun to take some pictures of their visitor? She let the bird perch on Andrew's finger and went to find her camera. With every photograph Hummy seemed to invite Teri to take closer pictures. She moved closer and closer to Hummy until the camera was within inches of the bird's head. Hummy didn't flinch. It was as if she was posing for the camera and saying, "Look at me, in the hand of a good friend."

Their last hour with Hummy was spent in wonderment over the events of that summer afternoon. Back in Teri's hand, Hummy was feeling strong enough to walk up and down on her fingers and around on her palm. Every once in a while, she fluttered her feathers and flapped her wings to test her strength. Teri could feel Hummy's heart drumming fast, steady and strong.

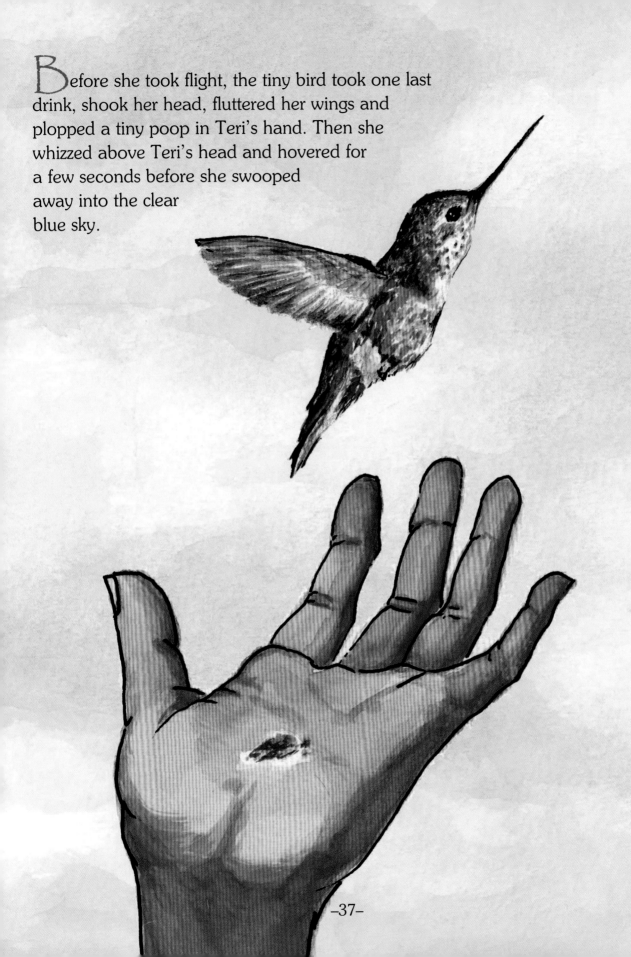

Before she took flight, the tiny bird took one last drink, shook her head, fluttered her wings and plopped a tiny poop in Teri's hand. Then she whizzed above Teri's head and hovered for a few seconds before she swooped away into the clear blue sky.

Teri and Andrew were happy to see her fly away, strong
and well. Four hours had passed, yet time seemed to
have stood still. Were it not for the lingering
tingling sensation in their hands from
feeling Hummy's heart beat
and the tickle of her tiny
claws, they might not
have believed the
last few hours
had been
real.

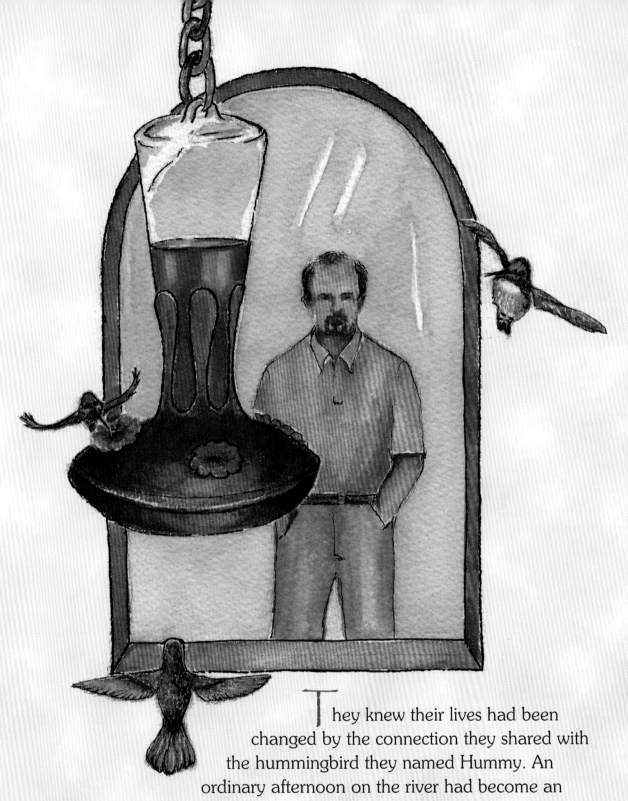

They knew their lives had been
changed by the connection they shared with
the hummingbird they named Hummy. An
ordinary afternoon on the river had become an
extraordinary day for all three of them.

Andrew wondered if they would *ever* see Hummy again. For days he
looked out their bedroom window at the hummingbird feeder, hoping to see her
come back to visit. Many hummingbirds of various colors came to drink at the
feeder, but not Hummy.

Then,
one day Andrew glanced out his window
and saw a hummingbird hovering right in front
of him. She was peering into their bedroom. He
could hardly believe his *eyes*. It was Hummy,
looking at him through the glass. Andrew pulled out
his binoculars to make sure the markings were the
same as hers. He had memorized them while
she was in his hands. It was her! No
question about it.

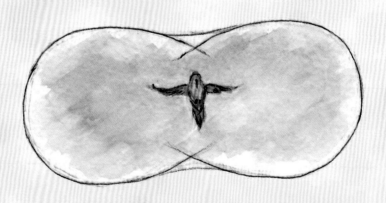

"Hummy
has come back to us!"
Andrew thought. After
looking in on them, their little
friend flew to the feeder and
perched on the edge while she
drank. No other hummingbird
had ever landed on the rim.
They always hovered around
the feeder in the air,
never coming to rest.

The bond Andrew and Teri had made with Hummy taught them to better appreciate the wonder of life, especially the strength that even the smallest creatures have.

From then on Hummy visited Andrew
and Teri often. Every time they saw her,
they were reminded of that very special
magical day.